Grades 3-

MYSTERY SCIENCE

The Case of the Missing Bicycle

Diego Patino &
Suzanna E. Henshon, Ph.D.
Illustrated by Michael Arnold

Prufrock Press Inc.
P.O. Box 8813
Waco, TX 76714-8813
Phone: (800) 998-2208
Fax: (800) 240-0333
http://www.prufrock.com

TABLE OF CONTENTS

ACKNOWLEDGMENTS

We would like to thank Linda Rowland, Dr. Donna Price Henry, and Dr. Myra Mendible of Florida Gulf Coast University for their support of this project. We express gratitude toward Meg Lieberman, Doug Bunch, Nina Sanders, Janice Patino, and Eduardo Patino for their advice and support. We are also grateful for the support and expertise of Kelly Dilworth, Jenny Robins, and Joel McIntosh of Prufrock Press.

Introduction

Mystery Science: The Case of the Missing Bicycle will get your students excited about school. This mystery science workshop promotes cooperation, teamwork, and active learning in a typical classroom setting.

Mystery Science: The Case of the Missing Bicycle is a real-life mystery that students can easily understand. While solving this mystery, your students will make deductions, analyze evidence, and develop higher order thinking skills.

As your students move through each activity in the workshop, they will learn the basic principles of scientific inquiry and develop an important foundation for scientific literacy. They will gain confidence in their ability to sort through and analyze competing information and they will learn to think about information and evidence with skepticism and reason.

WHY INQUIRY-BASED LEARNING?

The Mystery Science series for grades 3–4 was designed to meet the growing need in elementary school classrooms for hands-on, inquiry-based activities.

Students learn best when they engage in exploration and discovery. Inquiry-based learning is an effective, research-based approach to scientific instruction that encourages students to take charge of their own learning and think critically and creatively about the world around them.

By participating in hands-on, inquiry-based learning, your students will strengthen their ability to apply important science concepts to real world events. They will gain a richer appreciation for the subject matter that they are investigating, and they will learn how to think like real scientists.

ABOUT THE MYSTERY

Eleven-year-old John Smith discovers that his bicycle is missing just a few days after he received it as a birthday gift. Where is it? The culprit has left behind a minimal amount of evidence. Although the bicycle is eventually discovered in a ditch alongside the road, an important question remains: Who stole the bicycle?

After interviewing residents of the Bedford Heights neighborhood where the bicycle was stolen, detectives believe that five young suspects have a possible motive for taking the bicycle. Can they find the guilty person? Or will the cycle snatcher escape punishment and continue swiping bikes?

Students will examine Crime Scene 1 (the place from which the bicycle was taken), Crime Scene 2 (the place where the bicycle was found), and evidence found at these two settings. As they piece together the chain of events, examine evidence, and eliminate suspects, they will eventually discover the true identity of the cycle snatcher.

STANDARDS

Mystery Science: The Case of the Missing Bicycle aligns with the following National Science Education Standards for grades K–4 (National Research Council, 1996):

Content Standard A: As a result of activities in grades K–4, all students should develop:
- ➤ Abilities necessary to do scientific inquiry
  - Ask a question about objects, organisms, and events in the environment.
  - Plan and conduct a simple investigation.
  - Employ simple equipment and tools to gather data and extend the senses.
  - Use data to construct a reasonable explanation.
  - Communicate investigations and explanations.
- ➤ Understanding about scientific inquiry
  - Scientific investigations involve asking and answering a question and comparing the answer with what scientists already know about the world.
  - Scientists use different kinds of investigations depending on the questions they are trying to answer. Types of investigations include describing objects, events, and organisms; classifying them; and doing a fair test (experimenting).
  - Simple instruments such as magnifiers, thermometers, and rulers provide more information than scientists obtain using only their senses.
  - Scientists develop explanations using observations (evidence) and what they already know about the world (scientific knowledge). Good explanations are based on evidence from investigations.

- Scientists make the results of their investigations public; they describe the investigations in ways that enable others to repeat the investigations.
- Scientists review and ask questions about the results of other scientists' work.

Content Standard B: As a result of the activities in grades K–4, all students should develop an understanding of:
- ➢ Properties of objects and materials
  - Objects have many observable properties, including size, weight, shape, color, temperature, and the ability to react with other substances. Those properties can be measured using tools, such as rulers, balances, and thermometers.
  - Objects are made of one or more materials, such as paper, wood, and metal. Objects can be described by the properties of the materials from which they are made and those properties can be used to separate or sort a group of objects or materials.

TIMING

It takes approximately two and a half to three hours to complete the activities, examine all of the evidence, and solve the case. The case can easily be done during one day or divided into two separate class sessions. Although the timing for this Mystery Science workshop is flexible, it is recommended that you complete each of the activities in order.

PREPARATION AND ADAPTATIONS

This mystery scenario has been tested with children in grades 3–4 and is suitable for use in the classroom. If necessary, you can make minor modifications to the material to better suit the needs of your students. Although the crime scenes are ideally set up outside, you can also arrange the scenes in the hallway of your school or within your classroom.

As you get ready to present this workshop to your class, you will find that almost all of the materials that are required to stage this mystery are readily available from your classroom or home, or are provided as reproducible worksheets in this book. Additional materials have also been provided for you at the back of this book, including footprints for your crime scene (see Appendix A) and an optional vocabulary sheet (see Appendix B).

ASSESSMENT

At the back of this book, you will find a reproducible rubric for assessment (see Appendix C). Assess for understanding by collecting students' Mystery Science detective notebooks and surveying students' notes. You may also assess your students' interpersonal skills by observing how they cooperate with classmates during group work. Even if students do not identify the cycle snatcher (and solve the case), they may receive a positive assessment based upon their effort, cooperation, and attitude.

Inquiry-based activities can sometimes be challenging for students at this age to master and so you may have to subtly guide your students toward the right answers as they work through the activities in the book.

HOW TO USE THIS BOOK

Before using this book with your class, take the time to read through it from beginning to end. This workshop is most effective when you have time to prepare it carefully. Remember that your students will reap a myriad of educational benefits while chasing the elusive thief!

This book is divided into five, easy-to-follow sections: Preparing for the Investigation; Observing the Crime Scene; Evaluating the Crime Scene; Examining the Evidence; and Solving the Crime. As you move through the investigation, you will find detailed instructions for each activity, as well as corresponding student handouts. You may reproduce the handouts ahead of time or photocopy them as you go along.

For each activity, you also will find a short list of goals at the end of the activity's introduction. These goals summarize the scientific process skills and inquiry concepts that students will practice and gain exposure to in the activity.

Part One: Preparing for the Investigation

Allow several days to gather all of your materials. Once you have gathered your materials, set up the two crime scenes and the forensics lab before students arrive at school in the morning so that they can begin detective work immediately.

SETTING UP THE CRIME SCENES

On page 12 is a sample of what the two crime scenes should look like. Use the following instructions to construct similar crime scenes outside your school. Feel free to use your imagination and build on these ideas as you create your own version of the scenes.

If you would prefer to construct the crime scenes inside your classroom, rather than outdoors, see page 11 for alternative instructions.

Materials

- ➤ a bicycle (preferably child's size)
- ➤ yellow caution tape or string
- ➤ 6–8 chairs *or* 8–10 orange cones
- ➤ clear packing tape
- ➤ coins (dimes, nickels, and pennies)
- ➤ a separate bag of pennies
- ➤ a baseball card
- ➤ tissues
- ➤ a marble
- ➤ a backpack
- ➤ an age-appropriate young adult novel
- ➤ sheet of homework for the backpack (p. 59)
- ➤ footprints for the crime scene (see Appendix A on pp. 76–85)
- ➤ leaves and other natural objects (branches, sticks, rocks)
- ➤ mud
- ➤ water
- ➤ *optional*: two large sheets of butcher paper (approximately 6 × 8 feet)

Procedure

Before You Leave the Classroom:

1. Copy the footprints found on pages 76–85. Cut them out.
2. Copy p. 59 and place the homework in a backpack along with tissues, a bag of pennies, and an age-appropriate young adult novel.
3. Gather your materials together and bring them with you to the areas where you will stage your crime scenes.

At the Crime Scenes:

1. Pick an area outside of the classroom where you can safely stage the mystery without too much interruption. For best results, pick a grassy area outside of the school that is already muddy or that you can spray with a hose in order to create the illusion that it has just rained. You may also pour a bucket of water in a separate area where there is dirt and transport the mud to the grassy area. This will be Crime Scene 1.
2. Pick another grassy area nearby. If you can find a shallow ditch on your school campus that your students can safely enter and observe, then that would be ideal. If not, choose an area that is close to Crime Scene 1, but that is somewhat out of students' line of vision. This will be Crime Scene 2.
3. Dip the wheels of the bicycle in the mud and place the bicycle face down in the grass in the middle of Crime Scene 1. Let the bicycle lie there for several minutes, creating an impression in the grass that students can observe. If the bicycle fails to make a noticeable impression in the grass, don't worry. This isn't an important detail for the scene. You may simply point to the area later and tell students that this is where the bicycle was found.
4. Leave the baseball card, marble, and tissue somewhere near the bicycle and sprinkle coins (including several pennies) around the area. These artifacts will later become evidence for your students to analyze at the forensics lab.
5. Place the footprints at Crime Scene 1 in the order shown on the diagram on page 11 You may hold down the footprints with rocks so that the footprints stay in place or you may tape them to the grass.
6. Pick the bicycle up and ride away on it, steering the bicycle toward Crime Scene 2. If there is mud on the grass that the bicycle can drive through, use the muddy wheels to create tire track evidence on the ground. (This is difficult to do if the grass is completely dry.) Leave the bicycle at Crime Scene 2.

Mystery Science: The Case of the Missing Bicycle

7. Spread a trail of pennies leading from Crime Scene 1 to Crime Scene 2 alongside the bicycle tracks that you have just created.
8. At Crime Scene 2, cover the bicycle in leaves and other natural objects such as branches, sticks, and anything else that you can find.
9. Place a tissue next to the bicycle.
10. Place the backpack filled with the homework sheet, the novel, the bag of pennies, and the tissues near the bicycle but not directly next to it.
11. Place 3–4 chairs or 4–5 orange cones in a circle around Crime Scene 2. Surround the objects with yellow caution tape or string and secure with tape. Do the same for Crime Scene 1.

Anything Else?

➤ Make sure that the crime scene is not disturbed between the time when you set it up and when your students begin working on the case. This will require cooperation from all of the teachers, students, and the school staff. You may also want to get permission from your principal before you set up the scenes.
➤ If you are setting up your crime scenes inside, you may want to make the following alterations:
  • Choose two areas, either in the hallway outside your classroom, or on opposite ends of your classroom, to set up the scenes. Before you set up your crime scenes, consult with school officials to make sure that the crime scenes can remain intact long enough for your students to complete this activity.
  • Tape two large sheets of butcher paper together and place them in the corner that you have chosen for Crime Scene 1. Do the same for Crime Scene 2. Tape the footprints to the butcher paper. (If you want to make your crime scene look even more realistic, dip three sets of children's-size shoes in paint and spread them across the butcher paper. Be sure to measure and photocopy these prints, as well, so that students can examine them as evidence.)
  • Sprinkle the pennies from one scene to another in a clear path. Students will follow the pennies from Crime Scene 1 to Crime Scene 2.
  • If your classroom floor is tile and you have time to clean it up afterward, you may also make tire impressions on the floor by walking the bicycle through mud and riding it from one crime scene to another.

LAYOUT OF THE CRIME SCENES

The following diagrams show you how to prepare your crime scenes.

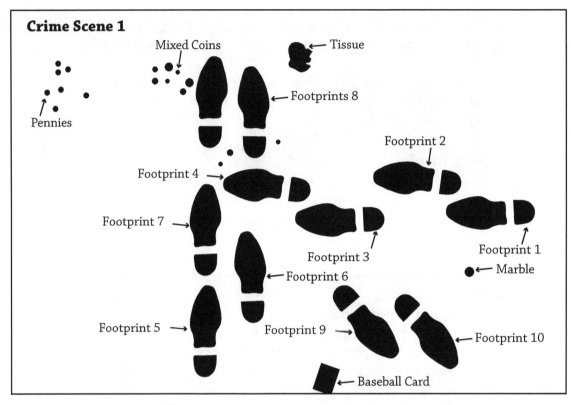

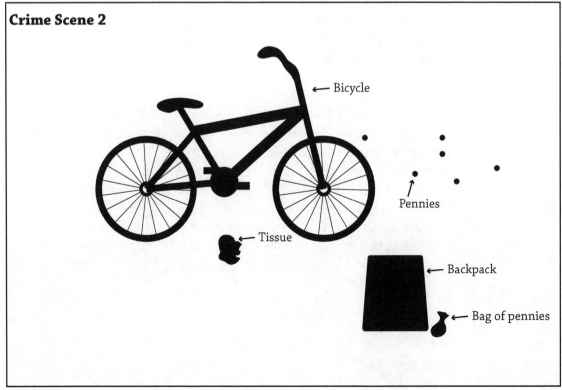

ASSEMBLING THE MYSTERY SCIENCE DETECTIVE NOTEBOOKS

On pages 26–40, you will find masters for the Mystery Science Detective notebooks (Student Handout C). If you wish, you may add a couple of blank pages to the backs of the notebook so that students have extra room for taking notes.

Materials

> Student Handout C
> stapler

Procedure

1. Duplicate copies of the notebook pages so that each student has one notebook.
2. Collate the notebooks so that the page numbers are in chronological order. Include extra pages at the end.
3. Staple the notebook pages together.

TRANSFORMING YOUR CLASSROOM INTO A FORENSICS LAB

If you are completing the workshop in one day, then you should prepare the forensics lab at the same time that you prepare the crime scene. If you are dividing the workshop into two days, then you may want to wait until the second day to set up the lab. That way, the timing for the collection of evidence will feel more realistic. Don't worry yet about the evidence for Station One. You will collect the physical evidence found at the crime scenes with the class. You may then add those items (sealed in plastic bags) to Station One right before your students enter the lab.

Materials

- two to three sets of latex or cotton gloves
- four magnifying glasses
- four to six 12-inch rulers
- one sheet of tracing paper per student
- 8 to 12 pencils
- two kitchen timers or stop watches
- one large, color photograph (preferably from a magazine) of a person engaging in an activity that can easily be described by students (e.g., sitting, standing, playing a sport). The subject's eye color, face shape, and hair color should be visible. Ideally, the subject will also be wearing at least one accessory such as a hat, a scarf, glasses, large jewelry, or anything else that students can describe).
- one sheet of construction paper
- one sheet per student of drawing paper
- glue or tape
- eight file folders
- one marker for labeling
- eight large sticky labels to place at the front of the file folders
- station instructions (pp. 47–53)
- suspects' footprints (pp. 54–58)
- a duplicate copy of the homework found at the crime scene (p. 59)
- suspects' signatures (p. 60)
- drawing of Jason's house (p. 61)
- eyewitness statements (pp. 62–65)
- suspects' statements (pp. 66–70)
- footprints found at the crime scene (pp. 76–85)

Procedure

1. Divide student workspaces into six crime lab stations.

2. Count the number of students in your class. You will divide your students into small groups of two to three later in the activity. Determine how many groups you will have.

3. Place the directions for each crime lab station (pp. 47–53) at the appropriate workspace.

4. Place two to three latex or cotton gloves at Station One. (Remember that some students may be allergic to latex and so you will want to check for allergies beforehand.)

5. At Station Two, place a copy of each person's footprints (pp. 54–58) in a file folder. Label the file folder, "Suspects' Footprints." Place copies of the footprints found at the crime scene (pp. 76–85) in a second file folder. Label the second file folder, "Evidence." Place two to three rulers and two magnifying glasses next to the file folders.

6. At Station Three, stack enough tracing paper for each student in the class to be able to use one sheet. You may want to add additional sheets of tracing paper to the stack just in case a student makes a mistake and needs to start over. Make a copy of the homework found at Crime Scene 2 (found on p. 59) and place it in a file folder. Label the folder, "Evidence." Make a copy of the suspects' signatures found on page 60, and cut them out so that you have five different handwriting samples. Place the signatures in a file folder, and label the folder, "Suspects' Handwriting Samples." Place two to three pencils, two magnifying glasses, and two to three rulers next to the file folders.

7. At Station Four, place a drawing of Jason's house (p. 61) in a file folder. Label the file folder, "How Observant Are You?" Place enough sheets of drawing paper for every student to use one sheet next to the file folder. Place a timer or a stopwatch next to the file folders.

8. At Station Five, place the eyewitness statements in a file folder. Label the file folder, "Eyewitnesses." Glue or tape the large, color photograph to a sheet of construction paper. Place the photograph in a second file folder. Label the second file folder, "How Good Is Your Memory?" Place a time or stopwatch next to the file folders.

9. At Station Six, place the suspect statements (pp. 66–70) in a file folder. Label the file folder, "Alibis."

Part Two: Observing the Crime Scene

ACTIVITY ONE

Read the newspaper story outlining the mystery.

Materials

- Student Handout A
- Student Handout B
- pencils

Procedure

1. Hand each student a copy of the newspaper story provided on page 18 (Student Handout A) and Student Handout B (pp. 21–23), which explains the challenge. If you wish, you may dramatize the fact that a crime has taken place in a nearby neighborhood called Bedford Heights and that the crime has still not been solved. You may also want to explain that a similar crime scene has been set up at your school so that students can help solve the case.
2. Explain to students that they will be working as crime scene investigators that day and that it will be their job to crack the case.
3. Ask students to listen closely as the newspaper story is read aloud, and to underline in pencil any information that seems like it could be important to the case. Remind students that they can always change their minds about key pieces of information later in the activity. Students may also underline or circle words that they do not know.
4. Read the newspaper story aloud. If you prefer that students actively practice their reading skills, you may also ask students to take turns reading the story to the class.
5. After you have finished reading the newspaper story aloud, read the paragraph on Student Handout B that introduces the class challenge.

Goals for This Activity

- Students will learn to listen carefully for clues and will practice sorting through information that may or may not be related to the mystery.

- Students will communicate their ideas and will strengthen their critical thinking and reading skills by underlining passages that they think could be important to the case.
- Students will expand their vocabulary and will learn important forensic science terms such as eyewitness, observation, and evidence.

THE BEDFORD BULLETIN

The Community Newspaper of Bedford Heights

Eleven-Year-Old's Bicycle Stolen on 8th Avenue and Cherry Hill Lane; Found in Ditch on the Side of Park Road

By Samson Case

Early Wednesday evening, 11-year-old John Smith walked into his living room and received a welcome surprise. Set against the wall next to a pile of birthday presents was a brand new bicycle with two shiny red bows tied around the handles. Smith jumped up and down in excitement and ran toward the new bicycle. He had wanted a new bicycle for a very long time. However, little did he know that just a few days later his bicycle would disappear!

According to investigators, John Smith's bicycle was taken on Saturday afternoon from a neighbor's lawn on Cherry Hill Lane and was later found in a low-lying ditch on Park Road, not far from where the bicycle disappeared. The bicycle was covered in debris, but it appeared to be in good condition. Investigators say that they are trying to piece together the chain of events that occurred before the bicycle was stolen.

According to John Smith, the last time that he rode his bicycle before it went missing was on Saturday morning, just before lunchtime. That morning, he rode his bicycle around the corner from his house on 8th Avenue to his friend Jason Worth's house on Cherry Hill Lane. He then left the bicycle on the stretch of lawn that was closest to the street.

"I thought about tying the bicycle to a nearby tree," said Smith when asked about the bicycle, "but I changed my mind because I figured that Bedford Heights is a safe neighborhood. Nothing ever happens here!"

After eating a grilled cheese sandwich that Mrs. Worth had made for him for lunch and spending a few minutes doing mathematics homework, Smith says that he looked outside the window at his bicycle around 1:30 p.m. and noticed that the bicycle was in a different position from where he left it.

"I didn't worry about it, though," said Smith. "I figured that maybe someone walking by had moved the bicycle out of the way since I did leave it pretty close to the street."

Smith said that he then went into the TV room to play video games with his friend and stayed there for the rest of the afternoon.

"We didn't stop playing video games until it was nearly time for dinner," remarked Jason Worth as he sat next to Smith on a park bench outside their elementary school. "We were so absorbed in the video games that we didn't even leave the room!"

When the two boys finally walked outside at 4:30 p.m., the bicycle was nowhere to be found. According to Worth, Smith gasped when he saw that the bicycle was missing and ran toward the spot where he had left it. He then covered his eyes and exclaimed, "What happened to my bicycle?" The two boys immediately went looking for it.

Virginia Borden, who lives across the street from Jason Worth, said that she was surprised when she saw the two boys run out of the house so close to suppertime. She said that she noticed around 4 p.m. that John Smith's bicycle was no longer on Jason Worth's lawn, but she didn't think anything of it because she assumed that Smith had gone home already.

"It was getting awfully late by then," remarked Mrs. Borden, who said that she was a friend of John Smith's family. "I know that Johnny's mother likes to have dinner on the table at 5 p.m. sharp every day and so I assumed that he must be home by then. I knew that it was getting close to suppertime because I was already hungry myself."

Mrs. Borden said that she went inside soon after she saw the two boys walk down the street out of eyesight. When asked if she saw someone come near the bicycle earlier that afternoon, she hesitated.

"No, no, I didn't see anyone," said Mrs. Borden slowly. Then she changed her mind. "Well, no that's not true, I have such a poor memory, you know. I did see some children come near the bicycle, several in fact, and I even saw one boy pick the bicycle up at one point, but he left without taking it."

Amy Sampson, who also lives across the street from Jason Worth, agreed. According

The kids are very nice to each other. You hardly ever see them fighting over their toys.

to Sampson, several children passed by the bicycle and showed interest in it. She said that she even saw more than one child pick the bicycle up by the handlebars.

"That didn't alarm me, though, because the kids in the neighborhood show interest in each other's toys all the time," noted Mrs. Sampson. "Many times they will even share their toys with one another. That's just how it is in this neighborhood. The kids are very nice to each other. You hardly ever see them fighting over their toys."

Sampson said that she did see one child pick the bicycle up and ride away on it, but she didn't know if that was the same person who took John Smith's bicycle without his knowledge. She then noted that she wasn't allowed to publicly say anything further about the subject because the information about the child riding the bike was part of an active investigation.

Paul Stillwell, who delivers mail to the neighborhood every afternoon, said that he ran into John Smith and Jason Worth on the corner of Cherry Hill Lane and Park Road around 4:45 p.m. According to Stillwell, the two boys said that they were looking for Smith's bicycle and asked him if he had seen it.

"I walked with the boys for several minutes and helped them look for the bike. They were following a muddy trail that looked like bicycle tracks and I suggested that they follow the coins that were nearby, as well. There were pennies all over the place. Eventually I had to return to my mail route and so I waved goodbye and wished them luck. About 30 minutes later, I saw the boys pointing to a ditch across from Park Road. I was running late, though, so I couldn't stop to help."

"The ditch was where we found the bicycle," said Jason Worth. "We were following the tire tracks and some coins that we had found on the ground when I looked over at the ditch and noticed something shiny in it. I pointed to the object and asked John what he thought it was and he stared at it for several minutes before he recognized it. It was hard to see because of all the leaves."

According to Jason Worth, Smith finally replied, "I think that's my bicycle!" and ran toward the spot where the object was hidden. As the two boys began to recover John's bicycle from the debris, Smith's mother suddenly called after him from the street.

"It was such bad timing!" recalled John Smith, who said that he was grounded for the rest of the weekend for not coming home on time. "Just as we began to wipe the leaves off of the bicycle, my mom and dad came running toward the ditch. They were really mad at me because I was late for dinner and I hadn't called. After my dad saw the bicycle, he called the police and they said that they would come to pick it up."

According to the Police Precinct Captain for the Bedford Heights neighborhood, Jaime Garcia, investigators searched the vicinity of Cherry Hill Lane and Park Road immediately after receiving the call from John's father.

"We are determined to stop the cycle snatcher in his or her tracks," said Precinct Captain Garcia. "Based upon the confidential clues and eyewitness statements that we have gathered so far, we believe the suspect is about five feet tall, between 10 and 12 years old, and lives in the Bedford Heights neighborhood."

According to Garcia, investigators have recently begun focusing their attention on children living in the neighborhood who had the opportunity and motivation to steal the bicycle. These children gave statements to the police, and a special crime unit, The Bike Busters, was formed to solve the crime. "It was difficult finding suspects in this case, but we have narrowed our search to five individuals," said Garcia.

The identities of the suspects have been kept anonymous in order to protect the suspects' privacy. "It is a sensitive case," Garcia noted, "and we are focusing our attention on creating a crime-free neighborhood. We have taken statements from several children, including those who are known to have touched the bicycle and children who are known for bullying. We are also looking at nontraditional suspects, including children who lost bike-riding privileges recently. Finally, we are working with the physical description of the suspect. We are trying to see if any child fits the profile described by eyewitnesses."

Can you help the Bedford Heights neighborhood solve the case of the missing bicycle? If we don't find out who stole John's bicycle soon, he or she will probably take another bike. So let's solve this case and stop the cycle snatcher right now!

THE CHALLENGE

As crime scene investigators, it will be your job to find out who took John's bicycle. Be careful not to jump to conclusions too early because sometimes you may accuse the wrong person. Think carefully about each piece of evidence that you find and don't forget to ask lots of questions. You never know, the person that you least suspect could turn out to be the one who stole John's bicycle!

STEPS YOU SHOULD FOLLOW

Think like a scientist: observe, inquire, analyze data, evaluate clues, self-assess, and communicate.

1. **Observe:** Use your senses (your sight, your hearing, your sense of smell, your ability to touch and feel) to collect information. Gather as much information as you can this way. You will then use this information to look for clues and evaluate facts that may help you solve the case.
2. **Inquire:** Follow your curiosity and ask questions about what you see. You never know, one small question that seems silly at the time may lead to an important answer!
3. **Analyze Data:** Collect facts and analyze them for clues. Carefully study the information that you have collected and look for sequences and patterns. Be sure to exercise patience because not all of the facts that you collect will help you solve the crime.
4. **Evaluate Clues:** Make inferences about the information that you have collected and decide whether a piece of

information is important or unimportant to the case. Piece together clues and determine whether you have enough reliable information to build a theory.

5. **Self-Assess:** Ask yourself every step of the way: What am I doing? Am I getting anywhere by doing this? If you are hitting a roadblock in your search for clues, ask yourself: Is there a better way to accomplish my goals for this activity? What can I do differently?

6. **Communicate:** Tell your classmates what you are doing and share your ideas. Listen to your classmates' ideas with an open mind and consider using their ideas in your investigation. After all, when it comes to solving problems, working together is often better than working alone.

TERMS YOU SHOULD KNOW

Investigator: A person who studies a problem or event by examining it and asking questions. For example: *The investigator tried to learn more about what may have happened to Mr. Mabry's missing tractor by reading newspaper articles about the crime and underlining clues.*

Eyewitness: Someone who sees an object or an event take place and reports on what he or she has seen. For example: *In one newspaper article, a 7-year-old eyewitness reported that she saw a man in a blue hat and red shirt drive the tractor down Main Street.*

Crime Scene: The location where a crime is believed to have taken place. For example: *Another newspaper article showed a photograph of the crime scene where the tractor was taken from Mr. Mabry's farm.*

Student Handout B

Observation: The act of gathering information about something by using one or more of the five senses such as hearing, touch, or sight. For example: *The investigator noticed a broken fence and a tall, green bush in the background of the photograph and recorded both of these observations in her notebook.*

Evidence: Anything that helps prove that an event took place or that a judgment or a conclusion is true. For example: *After comparing the photograph of the broken fence to a photograph that was taken of the tractor the day before it disappeared, the investigator marked the two photographs as evidence that the fence was not broken the day before the tractor was stolen.*

Culprit: The person who is responsible for committing a crime. For example: *The investigator wondered if the culprit who stole the tractor entered Mr. Mabry's farm by breaking apart a section of the fence.*

ACTIVITY TWO

Observe the crime scenes.

Materials

> ➤ Student Handout C
> ➤ pencils

Procedure

1. Hand each student a Mystery Science detective notebook (Student Handout C) and a pencil. Explain that the notebook is important because it will help them keep a record of their investigation.
2. Guide students toward Crime Scene 1 and tell them that this crime scene is a replica of the original crime scene in Bedford Heights where the bicycle was stolen. (Remember, Crime Scene 1 is where the bicycle was originally taken from, so there will be some evidence in this setting but *no bicycle.*) Your students will find a marble, a tissue, a baseball card, several coins, and footprints on the ground.
3. Ask students to silently use their observation skills to examine the crime scene. Encourage students to walk around and explore the scene, but remind them not to touch anything. Tell them that it's extremely important that they don't disturb any of the evidence or any other part of the crime scene.
4. Instruct students to write notes about what they observe in the spaces provided in the notebook and to sketch what they see. Remind students that their drawing doesn't need to be perfect. It just needs to show the basic outline of the crime scene, the location of the evidence, and anything else that they think may be important. Ask students to carefully label what they draw and circle items that could be used as evidence.
5. Remind students that some evidence might not be relevant to the case at hand and that they are simply making guesses at this point. Remind them that it is important to think carefully and analyze all possibilities before drawing conclusions.
6. Once students are finished drawing Crime Scene 1, point to the trail of pennies on the ground and ask students to follow the items of evidence to Crime Scene 2.
7. Ask students to silently observe Crime Scene 2 (which is a replica of the original crime scene in Bedford Heights) and carefully sketch the crime scene, circling items of interest.

8. Once students are finished sketching the scene, guide students back to Crime Scene 1 so that you can immediately begin Activity Two.

Goals for This Activity

> ➤ Students will practice observing and classifying objects in their environment.
> ➤ Students will absorb and synthesize information about the case through visual observation and analysis.
> ➤ Students will learn to identify important details by sketching the crime scene and taking notes about what they see.
> ➤ Students will learn to keep a record of their investigation.

MYSTERY SCIENCE DETECTIVE NOTEBOOK

Name: _____

Date: _____

AT THE CRIME SCENES

1. Record your observations of Crime Scene 1. What does the crime scene look like? Do you notice anything strange or out of place?

2. Draw what you see at Crime Scene 1 in the space below. Show the items that you discovered at the crime scene. Carefully label what you draw. Circle items that you believe could be used as evidence.

Student Handout C

3. Record your observations of Crime Scene 2. What does the crime scene look like? Do you notice anything strange or out of place?

4. Draw what you see at Crime Scene 2 in the space below. Show the items that you have discovered at the crime scene. Carefully label what you draw. Circle items that you believe could be used as evidence.

CLASS DISCUSSION

My notes:

_____

_____

_____

_____

_____

_____

_____

_____

_____

_____

_____

_____

_____

_____

_____

_____

_____

_____

IN THE LAB

Read the instructions provided at your station and record your observations.

STATION ONE

1. My notes and observations: _____

_____

_____

2. Read the instructions for sorting the evidence found at the crime scene and record your results.

Category One: _____

Items: _____

_____

Category Two: _____

Items: _____

_____

Category Three: _____

Items: _____

_____

Category Four: _____

Items: _____

_____

Category Five: _____

Items: _____

_____

3. Do you think the cycle snatcher dropped all of these items? Why or why not?

_____

_____

4. What inferences can you make about the following items' owner(s)? The first example has been done for you.

Pennies: *There are a lot of pennies here, including a whole bag of them, and so the owner of the pennies may have been collecting them.*

Tissues: _____

_____

Marble: _____

_____

Baseball card: _____

_____

Book: _____

_____

➢ Scientists often organize information that they are preparing to study by classifying objects and arranging them in groups.
➢ Remember: Not every item of evidence will help you solve the mystery. However, you should still evaluate each item of evidence that you find with equal care and attention. After all, you never know which items will help you solve the case!

STATION TWO

1. My notes and observations: _____

_____

_____

_____

_____

_____

2. Read the instructions for sorting the footprints found at the crime scene by appearance. How many sets of footprints did you find?

_____

3. Read the instructions for measuring the suspects' footprints. Record your conclusions about the size of the footprints found at the crime scene and the size of each suspects' footprints.

Footprints found at the crime scene: _____

_____

_____

_____

Carlos Garcia: _____

Andrew Landsman: _____

Katie Wong: _____

Norman Fine: _____

Padma Ali: _____

Student Handout C

4. Record your observations about the appearance of the footprints left at the crime scene in the space below. Do they match any of the suspects' footprints?

_____

_____

_____

_____

_____

_____

5. Determine who was in the vicinity of John's bicycle. Record your conclusion.

_____

_____

_____

_____

_____

_____

> ➤ Collecting data is an important part of being a scientist. Scientists often collect as much information as they can before they even begin to solve a problem.
> ➤ Although it's possible to gather valuable information using just one or more of the five senses (sight, hearing, touch, smell, or taste), scientists often use tools and instruments (such as rulers) to measure and record scientifically accurate data and perform experiments that other scientists can repeat.

STATION THREE

1. My notes and observations:

Mystery writer: _____

_____

Carlos Garcia: _____

_____

Andrew Landsman: _____

_____

Katie Wong: _____

_____

Norman Fine: _____

_____

Padma Ali: _____

_____

2. My examination:

Mystery writer: _____

Carlos Garcia: _____

Andrew Landsman: _____

Katie Wong: _____

Norman Fine: _____

Padma Ali: _____

➤ This procedure is called forensic *graphology*. Forensic scientists use to help them analyze a person's unique handwriting style.

➤ Try comparing your handwriting with your partner's handwriting. Do your letters look the same? Everyone has a personal handwriting style that is uniquely their own. Some people form large, loopy letters that are close together, while others form small, narrow letters that are spaced widely apart. Although it's possible to alter your handwriting style, the overall appearance of your handwriting will always be uniquely yours.

STATION FOUR

1. Read the instructions provided at your station and record the results in the space below.

_____

_____

_____

_____

_____

2. Read the instructions provided at your station and write down every detail that you remember from the drawing of Jason's house.

_____

_____

_____

_____

_____

3. Did you miss any details? If so, what details did you miss?

_____

_____

_____

_____

_____

5. Study your drawings of the two crime scenes. Notice any patterns or noteworthy details? Record your observations in the space below.

_____

_____

_____

> ➤ Forensic scientists sketch crime scenes firsthand while they are on location because they know that they can't always trust their memories later on. For most people, it's hard to remember every detail from a complicated scene, even if you have a good memory. You may remember some details about the scene a day or two later (or maybe even a few minutes later), but you can easily forget others that may be crucial to solving the case.
>
> ➤ For any investigation that you are conducting, it's always a good plan to sketch everything that you see and take lots of notes so that you can review them later.

STATION FIVE

1. Contradictions: _____

_____

_____

2. Similarities: _____

_____

_____

3. Use the space below to write down every detail that you can remember about the photograph.

_____

_____

_____

_____

4. Did you have a hard time remembering details from the photograph? Why or why not?

_____

_____

5. Did your memory appear crystal clear or fuzzy when you tried to visualize the photograph?

_____

_____

6. Were all of your recollections accurate? If not, which details were incorrect?

_____

_____

_____

_____

> ➢ Forensic scientists know that they can't always trust their eyewitnesses to be 100% reliable. An eyewitness may be biased, or distracted, or his or her memory may be poor. Sometimes an eyewitness may even have a good memory, but still have trouble accurately remembering an event. In court cases, eyewitnesses often get details, particularly physical details, confused. That why it's always a good idea to approach eyewitness statements with a healthy dose of skepticism!

> ➢ Forensic scientists look for similarities in eyewitness statements in order to corroborate facts and details. If two eyewitnesses say that something is true, then the investigator is more likely to believe them and use their statements as reliable evidence.

STATION SIX

My notes and observations:

_____

_____

_____

_____

_____

_____

_____

_____

_____

_____

_____

_____

_____

➢ It's important to remember when evaluating suspect statements that the suspects might not always be telling the truth. He or she may attempt to slant his or her story, promote a favorable storyline, or alter or make up events that never really occurred.

➢ It's also important to remember that suspects may provide valuable information about other suspects. Always keep a lookout for clues when reading statements. You never know, it may help you solve the case!

MY CONCLUSIONS

Who: _____

What: _____

_____

_____

Where: _____

_____

_____

When: _____

_____

_____

Why: _____

_____

_____

How I Know: _____

_____

_____

ACTIVITY THREE

Measure the crime scene and gather evidence for the forensics lab.

Materials

➢ measuring tape
➢ rulers (optional)
➢ Student Handout C
➢ latex or cotton gloves (one pair)
➢ clear plastic bags

Procedure

1. Ask students to take turns helping you measure the crime scenes using measuring tape. One volunteer may hold one end of the tape and the other may hold the other end as you read the measurements aloud to the class. If you wish, you may ask a third volunteer to read the measurements aloud.
2. Ask students to guide you as you measure the scenes. Have them tell you what to measure. Make sure that you measure the footprints before completing the activity.
3. As you follow students' directions, ask students why they think you should measure particular areas of the crime scenes.
4. Instruct students to write down the measurements in the notetaking sections of their notebooks.
5. Remind students that not all of the measurements will be useful in solving the crime and that it's possible that none of the measurements will be useful.
6. After you have finished taking measurements of both crime scenes, put on a pair of gloves and make a point of carefully collecting all of the items of evidence, except for the footprints, and placing them in plastic bags.
7. As you gather evidence, explain to your students what you are doing and why you are doing it. Feel free to read the following statement to your class or to paraphrase it in your own words:

> When you are solving a mystery, it is important to gather evidence and to study it carefully. In this case, we have many different kinds of evidence. First, we have several footprints that might be connected to the cycle snatcher. We also have some physical items such as the baseball card, the marble, the backpack, and the coins that also might be connected to the culprit. But you should

remember that it is possible that these items don't belong to the cycle snatcher or to anyone else who is involved in the case at hand. As detectives, it will be your job to sift through these items of evidence and determine whether or not they will help you solve the mystery.

8. Once the class is finished gathering evidence, divide students into small groups and ask them to freely discuss their ideas about the case for five minutes. As your students discuss the activity, you may use this opportunity to leave the evidence that you have just collected from the crime scenes at Station One in the forensics lab.

Optional Activity. If you have time, you may distribute rulers or measuring tape to students (divided in pairs) and allow them to measure the crime scene themselves.

Goals for This Activity

➢ Students will practice using a simple instrument (measuring tape or ruler) to conduct their investigation.
➢ Students will learn to gather and record data that may or may not help them solve the case.
➢ Students will make guesses about what parts of the crime scene should be measured.
➢ Students will communicate their ideas to their peers.

Part Three: Evaluating the Crime Scene

ACTIVITY FOUR

Record crime scene observations and discuss.

Materials

- ➤ Student Handout C
- ➤ 1–2 large sheets of butcher paper
- ➤ 1 black marker
- ➤ 1 red marker

Procedure

1. Instruct students to return to their desks and turn their Mystery Science Detective Notebooks to page 29. Ask students to take detailed notes of the discussion that is about to take place.
2. Explain that collaboration is important in a scientific investigation and that students should listen closely to their classmates' observations. You should also explain that taking detailed notes of the discussion is important because one student's observation may help the rest of the class crack the case.
3. Discuss what the students know and don't know about the mystery at this point in the investigation. Ask students to reflect on what they learned from observing the crime scenes firsthand.
4. Ask each student to offer at least one detail that he or she noticed at the crime scenes. Instruct students to write down their classmates' answers in Mystery Science Detective Notebooks.
5. Discuss the parts of the crime scenes that should be considered evidence. Remind students that it is okay to make mistakes at the beginning of the investigation and that it is important not to draw conclusions too early.
6. On a large sheet of butcher paper, list the items of evidence found at the crime scenes as they come up in your discussion. Separate the items into two lists, one for each location. (You may want to write the second list on a separate sheet of butcher paper.) Make sure that you list the items inside the backpack in addition to the other items of evidence. List the backpack as an independent object of evidence and then list the individual items found inside the backpack underneath it.

7. Ask students if they notice any patterns or repeating objects between the two lists. (Students should notice that there were pennies and tissues at both crime scenes. Students should also notice that there were tissues and a bag of pennies inside the backpack.)
8. Using a red marker, circle the recurring items of evidence.
9. Ask students to guess the significance of these recurring items. (Students should infer that the presence of the tissues and the pennies at both crime scenes must mean that these items of evidence were likely dropped by the cycle snatcher. Students should also infer that the presence of the tissues and the bag of pennies inside the backpack must mean that the cycle snatcher likely dropped the backpack, as well.
10. Explain to students that by making these guesses about the items of evidence found at the scene, they are generating hypotheses. Write down students' guesses on the chalkboard or on another sheet of butcher paper and label students' guesses as, "Hypothesis 1," "Hypothesis 2," "Hypothesis 3," and so on. Explain that making a hypothesis and testing it throughout the investigation is an important part of inquiry-based science.

Some Guided Questions for Discussion

1. Why was it important not to disturb the evidence that we found at the crime scene?
2. What do you think could have happened if we touched or moved some of the evidence before we recorded it in our notebooks?
3. Why was it important for us to draw and measure the crime scene?
4. What do we know so far based on the evidence left at the crime scene?
5. What don't we know?

Goals for This Activity

➢ Students will share their observations about the crime scene with the class and will communicate their ideas about what should and should not be considered evidence.
➢ Students will reflect more deeply upon what they have observed by participating in a class discussion.
➢ Students will think critically about what they know and don't know about the case so far.
➢ Students will identify patterns and make inferences as a group.
➢ Students will generate hypotheses that they will later test in the forensics lab.

Part Four: Examining the Evidence

ACTIVITY FIVE

Analyze the evidence found at the crime scene.

Materials

> ➤ See pages 14–15 for a detailed list of station materials
> ➤ Student Handout C

Procedure

1. Guide students to the crime lab stations that you have set up in the classroom. Explain that the items that they collected at the crime scene have been placed at this secure forensics lab so that they can be examined for clues.
2. Tell students that it will be their job as crime scene detectives to not only sort through and analyze the evidence found at the crime scene, but also to read through suspect and witness statements in order to determine who may have committed the crime.
3. Break students into small groups and tell them that they are going to work together to examine the evidence and answer the specific questions that appear in their Mystery Science Detective Notebooks.
4. Tell students that they will find all of the materials that they need at each station, as well as an instruction sheet. Remind students that it is very important that they read and follow the instructions. Explain that if real crime scene investigators do not follow the proper steps, the results can lead them away from the true culprit.
5. Assign each group to a crime lab station and have them follow the directions for that station. When finished with one station, allow the groups of students to go to other stations. Tell students that it does not matter in what order the stations are completed. If all the stations are full, ask students to read through their notes while they wait for another station to open up.
6. Remind students to bring their detective notebooks to each station so that they can answer questions and keep track of the results of their experiments.
7. Walk around to supervise students' work. Guide students to a less crowded station if one area becomes too congested.

Goals for This Activity

➤ Students will strengthen their critical thinking and observational skills as they conduct their investigations.

➤ Students will build an important foundation for scientific literacy by engaging in activities that teach them to approach problems with skepticism and reason.

➤ Students will practice sorting through competing information and will improve their ability to synthesize large quantities of information.

➤ Students will increase their understanding of forensic science.

STATION ONE:
SORT THE EVIDENCE

1. Put on the gloves provided for you at the station. Carefully take the items of evidence out of the plastic bags and examine each item. Note the appearance of the item and the potential use for it. Record your observations on p. 30 in your Mystery Science Detective Notebook.

2. Carefully sort the items by category. For example, you may classify the marble and the baseball card as toys or you may choose to classify them as hobbies. You must divide the items into five separate categories. In the space provided in your notebook, write down the categories that you have created, and list the items in each category.

3. Return the items to their original bags. Then, take off your gloves and put the gloves back where you found them so that the next team may use them.

4. Answer questions 3–4 in your notebook.

STATION TWO:
FOLLOW THE FOOTPRINTS

1. Using the magnifying glass provided for you at the station, examine the footprints found at the crime scene. Observe the footprints' shape and their appearance. Note the grooves left by the shoes. Record your observations on page 32 in your notebook.
2. Sort the footprints by appearance. Count how many groups you just made. Record your observation in your notebook.
3. Measure each of the suspects' footprints. Record your measurements in your notebook.
4. Compare your measurements to the measurements that you recorded at the crime scene. Record your observations in your notebook.
5. Compare examples of the footprints that you discovered at the crime scene with the footprints of the suspects. Record your observations in your notebook. (Remember, you are supposed to match the footprints based on shoe size and appearance.)
6. Determine who was in the vicinity of John's bicycle. Record your conclusions in your notebook.

STATION THREE:
EXAMINE THE HANDWRITING

1. Inside the file folder labeled, "Evidence," you will find a duplicate copy of the sheet of homework that you found at Crime Scene 2. Using a magnifying glass provided for you at your station, observe the handwriting on the sheet. Note the size and appearance of the handwriting. Record your observations on page 34 of your Mystery Science Detective Notebook.

2. Inside the file folder labeled, "Suspects' Handwriting Samples," you will find 5 signatures belonging to the suspects. Using the magnifying glass, observe the handwriting for each signature. Note the size and appearance of the handwriting. Record your observations in your notebook.

3. Take a sheet of tracing paper and place it on top of the sheet of homework.

4. Choose two words from the sheet. Using a pencil, draw a large box around the words and then write "Mystery Writer" above the box. The box should look like this:

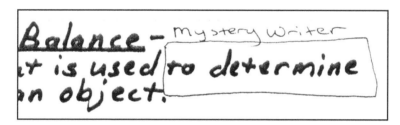

5. Draw a dot on the top of each letter, directly in the middle of the letter. Do the same for the bottom of the letter. Then connect the dots. Your letters should look like this:

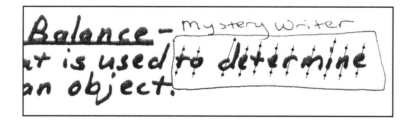

6. Hold the sheet of tracing paper in front of you and observe whether the lines that you have just made slant to the left, to the right, or are straight. Record your answer in your notebook in the space marked, "My examination."

7. Choose a suspect from the pile of oaths, and place the same sheet of tracing paper over the suspect's signature. Draw a box around the signature and write the suspect's name above the box.

8. Just as you did with the sheet of homework, draw a dot on the top of each letter and on the bottom of each letter. Make sure that your dots are directly in the middle of the letter. Connect the dots.

9. Hold your sheet of tracing paper in front of you, and determine whether the lines that you just made slant to the left, to the right, or are straight. Record your answer next to the suspect's name in the space marked, "My Examination."

10. Repeat this procedure with each signature.

STATION FOUR: STUDY THE CRIME SCENES

1. Without looking at your notebook, sketch both crime scenes from memory on the drawing paper provided at the station for 2 minutes. Time it!

2. Open your notebook to pages 27 and 28. Review your original sketches of the crime scenes. Did you miss anything? Record your answer on page 35 in your notebook.

3. Study the drawing of Jason's house for 20 seconds. Time it! When the buzzer goes off, quickly write down every detail that you can remember without looking at the drawing.

4. Flip the drawing over. Did you miss anything? Record your answer in your notebook.

5. Study your drawings of the two crime scenes. Note the objects and their placement in the scene. Look for any patterns or noteworthy items. Are there any objects that appear at both crime scenes? Record your answer in your notebook.

STATION FIVE:
TALK TO EYEWITNESSES

1. Take out the photograph provided for you in the folder labeled, "How Good Is Your Memory?" Study the photograph for one minute. Time it! When the buzzer goes off, return the photograph to the folder and put it aside. (Remember that this photograph has nothing to do with the case at hand. You are observing the photograph as part of an experiment.)

2. Read the statements from the eyewitnesses. These statements will help you determine what happened on the day that John's bicycle was stolen.

3. Are there any contradictions between the statements? Record your answer on page 37 in your notebook.

4. Are there any similarities or repeated facts in the witness statements? Record your answer in your notebook.

5. Return the eyewitness statements to the folder labeled, "Eyewitnesses."

6. Without looking at it, think about the photograph that you studied at the beginning of the activity. Don't peek! Write down every detail that you can remember about the person in the photograph. Write down what the person was doing, the color of his or her hair, the color of his or her eyes, and the shape of his or her face. Write down what kind of clothing the person was wearing in the photograph, the color of his or her clothing, and whether or not he or she was wearing glasses.

7. Answer questions 4–6 on pages 37 and 38 in your Mystery Science Detective Notebook.

STATION SIX:
RECORD ALIBIS

1. Read each statement sheet.
2. Record notes on what you have learned about each suspect on page 39 in your Mystery Science Detective Notebook.

CARLOS' FOOTPRINT

ANDREW'S FOOTPRINT

KATIE'S FOOTPRINT

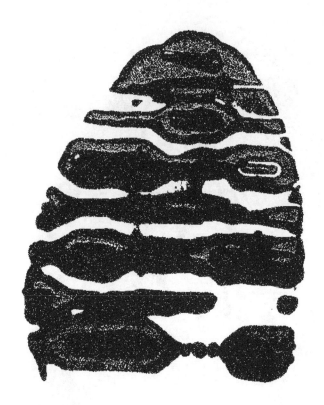

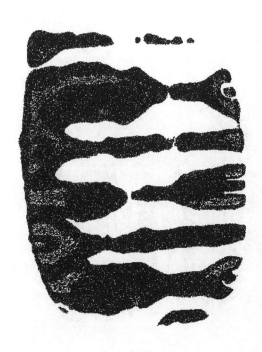

NORMAN'S FOOTPRINT

PADMA'S FOOTPRINT

SHEET OF HOMEWORK

Test Tube -
A long glass tube that has one
end open with the other end
rounded. It can be used for heating,
mixing, or collecting chemicals.
Because it has a rounded bottom
and cannot stand on its own, it usually
needs to be kept in a rack.

Thermometer -
A device used to measure temperature.
It contains mercury or colored
alcohol, which expands and rises in
the thermometer as the temperature
increases. Thermometers measure
temperatures in Celsius or Fahrenheit,
or both. Some current thermometers
provide digital readings.

Triple Beam Balance -
A balance that is used to determine
the mass of an object.

SUSPECTS' SIGNATURES

Carlos Garcia

Katie Wong

Norman Fine

Andrew Landsman

Padma Ali

EYEWITNESS STATEMENT
MRS. VIRGINIA BORDEN

I live across the street from the Worth household and am close friends with the Smiths. I saw Jimmy riding his bicycle after school earlier in the week. He seemed so proud of his new bicycle! Jimmy's such a nice boy. Hm? What's that, dear? Oh, did I say Jimmy? I meant Johnny. Johnny's the one with bicycle! I'm old, dear. My memory's not what it used to be!

On the day that Jimmy, I mean Johnny, lost his bicycle, I spent most of the afternoon on my porch working on my knitting. We have had such nice weather lately! Right now, I'm knitting a sweater for my dog, Charlie. He gets cold at night and needs something warm while he sleeps.

I believe that I saw Johnny leave his bicycle on the lawn across the street sometime in the morning. I remember that I was hungry at the time and so I must not have had breakfast yet. If that's true then it must have been really early in the morning, perhaps close to 8 a.m. I never eat my breakfast past 8:30 a.m. and so that must have been when Johnny left his bicycle across the street.

I noticed an awful lot of kids come up to the bicycle throughout the morning and afternoon. It seemed a bit suspicious to me, to tell you the truth. I can spot these things you know.

I saw one little boy come near the bicycle and he looked very suspicious. I believe he was blonde. Yes, he was blonde with hair that was so long that it went down past his ears! He was wearing a sleeveless T-shirt too. He looked very suspicious indeed!

EYEWITNESS STATEMENT
MRS. AMY SAMPSON

I live across the street from Jason Worth and spent much of that Saturday outside. I was watching my children as they played in our driveway. I saw several cars drive by but nothing out of the ordinary.

Around 11:30 a.m., I saw John place his new bicycle in front of Jason's house before heading inside to play.

I saw several boys walking down the street. The boys pointed to the bicycle and were very interested in riding it. One boy even held the bicycle by the handlebars. I didn't see his face, but he was wearing a long-sleeved T-shirt and a baseball cap. He didn't take the bicycle though. The boys moved away quickly and left the bicycle alone.

Out of the corner of my eye, I saw a child heading toward the bicycle around 3 p.m. This person was wearing an orange sweatshirt and ran fairly quickly. I couldn't tell if it was a girl or boy, but the child had short hair and was slim.

This child ran up to the bicycle, picked it up, and quickly rode away. At the time I didn't think too much of it. For all I knew, it might have been one of John Smith's friends. Children share their bicycles all the time, and it's not exactly something you call the police about. So when the boys began looking for the bicycle, I was surprised. Had the bike *really* been stolen? Was it possible someone had borrowed the bicycle and meant to return it later?

I pointed the boys in the direction that the child ran, but, unfortunately, I couldn't provide more specific details since I didn't recognize the child from afar.

EYEWITNESS STATEMENT
MR. PAUL STILWELL

I deliver the mail every afternoon. I know the neighborhood pretty well, and so I was surprised to see a brand-new bicycle left at the edge of the lawn. If I were 10 years old, I probably would have taken the bicycle for a spin myself.

As I delivered mail that day, I didn't notice anything out of the ordinary. Mothers were watching their children, and kids were running up and down the street. I was surprised that the owner of the bicycle left it so close to the street; most children park their bikes close to the house so people passing by aren't tempted to take them. But I just went about my business delivering mail.

I walked down the other side of the street to deliver some more mail, and it didn't seem like anything was wrong. The bicycle was gone, but I figured the owner had come back and removed it. I never expected it to be stolen.

Two boys approached me, and one boy asked, "Have you seen my bike? I left it right there."

"The bike on the edge of the grass?" I asked.

"Yes, that's the one," the boy said. "Have you seen it?"

"The last place I saw it was right there," I said, pointing to the lawn. "Did someone take it?"

The boy nodded, and that's when I realized that his bike had been stolen. I helped look for the bike for several minutes and even pointed the boys toward some coins on the ground. Then I had to complete my route. I was happy to hear the boys later found the bicycle in a ditch at the end of the street. But the cycle snatcher is still running loose. My guess is that other children who live in the neighborhood will have their bicycles stolen in the future, and it will create a less friendly neighborhood for everyone.

EYEWITNESS STATEMENT
MISS ANNA STEIN

I live across the street from the ditch on Park Avenue. I was working on my college applications at my dining room table when I looked out the window and saw a kid riding a bicycle near the ditch. The kid was riding so close to the ditch that I was afraid that the bicycle was going to slip and fall into the ditch. I didn't think anything of the bicycle, but I did think it was weird that the kid was riding the bike on the grass rather than on the sidewalk. That can be dangerous because the ground is uneven.

The kid had short hair, but I couldn't see the kid's face because the bicycle was moving too fast. The kid was wearing jean shorts and an orange sweatshirt.

Well . . . I think that the kid was wearing jean shorts. I definitely remember the orange sweatshirt. It was such a bright color orange that you couldn't miss it.

The kid was carrying a backpack too. I think the backpack was blue. Or maybe it was purple. I don't remember. I only saw the kid for a couple seconds to tell you the truth. I just remember the orange sweatshirt. I hate the color orange. I want to be a fashion writer someday and so fashion is very important to me.

SUSPECT STATEMENT
CARLOS GARCIA

I love bicycles! I've always wanted a bike. As I walked by Jason's house that afternoon, I saw Mrs. Borden sitting across the street. I tried to wave, but she wasn't paying attention. She seemed really absorbed in her knitting. I was about to take the bike for a quick spin when I realized that I should get permission from John first.

Plus, I was late for baseball practice anyway and so I didn't really have time. I love baseball. I could play baseball all day. I've been collecting baseball cards for years and now I have three binders full of cards. Lately, I've also begun collecting pennies. I have a bet with Katie, Norman, and Padma over who can collect the most pennies in the neighborhood by Christmas. I think I'm going to win. I have a pretty big collection.

I'm really sorry about John's bicycle. He should have been more generous about letting people ride it though. Then maybe someone wouldn't have stolen it. I asked John if I could ride his bike a few days earlier, and he refused. It bothered me a little, and I probably would have taken the bike out myself if I hadn't seen Mrs. Borden sitting there. When I started to walk over to the bicycle, I saw Mrs. Borden look up from her knitting and stare at me. I waved, but she just frowned and looked back down at her lap. I don't think she likes me.

Later that afternoon I was shocked to learn that the bicycle had been stolen. I helped Jason and John search for it for a little bit, but then I had to go. I'm happy the bike was found, but I'm very upset it was stolen in the first place.

SUSPECT STATEMENT
NORMAN FINE

I wish my parents would buy me a new bicycle. My bicycle was stolen from our garage a year ago. Because my parents are going through financial troubles, there isn't a lot of money to spend on special items. So I've been driving around on Dad's ancient bicycle, dreaming about the bicycle I lost.

When I was walking by the Worths' house with my friends, I saw the bicycle and thought about taking it for a spin. I knew it belonged to John because he's a friend of mine. John knows how much I miss my bike, and he even allowed me to ride his bike down the street a few weeks ago. So when I picked the bicycle up by the handlebars, I didn't think he would mind.

But after moving the bicycle off the lawn, I decided not to ride it around the neighborhood and so instead I tried to put it back where I found it. It isn't right to take John's bike without his permission. I am saving my allowance to buy another bike. I was surprised John left it out like that; we usually park our bikes closer to the house when we visit a friend.

I was *really* shocked when John's bike was stolen. I knew it meant a lot to him and so I felt badly about it. But I was working my paper route that afternoon, and I didn't have time to help search for it. Plus, I had a cold and was looking forward to just going home and taking it easy. I like to read when I'm sick because it's a restful activity. I still have a cold actually. It's been going around. Half the people in my math class have colds right now!

SUSPECT STATEMENT
PADMA ALI

I'd love to have my bike back! This past week I received a really bad report card—mostly C's and D's. So Mom and Dad grounded me, and I'm not allowed to ride my bicycle.

It doesn't make much sense that I can't ride my bike anymore. It's good exercise, and it doesn't interfere with my schoolwork. I don't really like any other sports. Riding my bike is the best exercise I can get. But Mom and Dad told me that I'm not allowed to ride my bike until my grades improve. So I'm stuck walking everywhere.

On the day that John's bicycle went missing, I spent most of the day reading indoors. I did walk by Jason's house before lunch and saw John's new bike on Jason's lawn. I couldn't help admiring it when I saw it. I *really* wanted to ride that bike. But I knew that if I was caught on someone else's bicycle, I'd get into even more trouble than I'm in at the moment.

I felt badly when the bike was stolen. Our neighborhood is a great place to live. People leave their houses unlocked. We trust each other. It really bothered me to hear that someone broke that trust.

I can't wait to ride again. I've been working hard (and have stayed away from texting on my cell phone) and my grades are steadily improving. In a few weeks, I hope to get my wheels back!

SUSPECT STATEMENT
ANDREW LANDSMAN

I own these streets. Some kids call me a bully, but I'm not *that* bad. I just like to be in charge of things. Of course, sometimes when I see a kid playing with a toy I like, I take it away from him.

John Smith got a great bike for his birthday—a nicer bike than my parents would ever buy for me. I couldn't help admiring it, and I was hoping for an opportunity to ride it around the neighborhood. When I asked, he wouldn't let me ride it.

On the day John's bicycle disappeared, I was at my cousin's house more than 4 miles away. We were watching reruns of *Survivor* from 3 to 6 that afternoon. So I clearly wasn't involved.

Nevertheless, I thought it was pretty dumb that he left his bike out like that. If you have the nicest and most expensive bike in the neighborhood, you don't leave it out on at the edge of a lawn. *Anyone* could have taken that bike; I'm surprised he got it back!

Maybe he'll be more careful next time. But the whole situation was caused by John's laziness. Who would leave his bike outside near the street? It's not the thief's problem; John needs to take *better* care of his stuff!

SUSPECT STATEMENT
KATIE WONG

I like riding my bike around the neighborhood with Padma. I have a mountain bike and I love feeling the breeze blowing through my hair. My best friend, Padma, and I used to ride our bikes all around town.

But then last week we received some bad news. Padma had a lousy report card, and her parents decided to take her bike away.

Padma has been stuck in her house ever since. All we are allowed to do when her parents are at home is read and play marbles. It's been a bummer spring for me, but I've found ways to get around it.

Padma's parents forbid her to ride *her* bike. They never said Padma couldn't ride *another* bike. A couple days ago I lent Padma *my* bike. I even gave her sunglasses as a disguise.

Padma's parents never found out that she rode my bike. I was surprised that we weren't caught. So I thought of other fun things that we could do in the time between when Padma gets out of school and her parents come home from work. You might think I'm mischievous, but it's fun fooling adults sometimes. It sure beats doing homework!

I was sorry to hear about John's bicycle. That's too bad.

On the day that John's bicycle was stolen, I went over to Padma's house and we read for a little bit and did homework. It was pretty boring. I had a cold though so I needed the rest.

After I left Padma's house later that afternoon, I was really tired of sitting around. I decided to take a walk around the neighborhood. I can't wait for Padma to be able to ride her bicycle again. My life is so boring right now!

Part Five: Solving the Crime

ACTIVITY SIX

Chart results.

Materials

- ➤ large paper for charting the results of the investigation
- ➤ marker for recording information
- ➤ tape
- ➤ Student Handout C

Procedure

1. Once each group has finished completing all of the stations, have students return to their desks and ask them to review their notes.
2. Tell students that they are going to discuss their results as a group and work together to solve the mystery. Remind students that sharing information and working together as a team is an important part of conducting a scientific investigation.
3. Hang a piece of butcher paper on the wall and label it, "Results." Record students' answers on the chart.
4. Ask students to review their notes from the suspect statements and from the footprints station. Then, ask students if they can make any educated guesses based on the information at hand. (At the minimum, students should eliminate the suspects who were not in the vicinity at the time that the bicycle disappeared.) In order to display the students' answers on the chart, you may wish to write down each of the suspects' names and then draw a line through each suspect as you eliminate them.
5. Ask students to analyze suspects' motives. Ask students if it's possible to eliminate any of the suspects that are still remaining based on lack of motive.
6. On a separate section of the butcher paper, write down the names of each of the remaining suspects next to one another in a horizontal line. Draw a line underneath each name and ask students to list what they know about each suspect.
7. Bring students' attention to the chart that they made during Activity Four. Ask students if they can use that information to eliminate any suspects based on the information that they know now.

8. Allow students to offer their guesses for who the culprit(s) may be. Write down their answers on the board and then discuss.
9. As a class, come up with a hypothesis for what really happened to John's bicycle. You may take a vote in order to determine the class hypothesis.
10. Ask students to fill in the last page of their Mystery Science Detective Notebooks ("My Conclusions").

Goals for This Activity

➢ Students will review their work and reflect on their experiences.
➢ Students will share their ideas with the class and compare their results.
➢ Students will analyze the forensic evidence and discern between relevant evidence and unconnected information.
➢ Students will work together to solve the mystery.

Anything Else?

➢ Students should note that Katie, Carlos, and Norman's footprints were found at Crime Scene 1. They should eliminate Padma because her footprints were not found at the scene and they should eliminate Andrew because he was in another part of town.
➢ Students also should note that Carlos is the most likely owner of the baseball card and that the pennies could potentially belong to Katie, Carlos, Norman, or Padma because they were all collecting pennies.
➢ Students should note that the tissues could potentially belong to Katie or Norman because they both had colds.
➢ Students should note that the book could potentially belong to Katie, Norman, or Padma because they all mentioned reading that day.
➢ Ideally, students will identify Katie as the cycle snatcher by linking her to the handwriting found on the sheet of homework and to the footprints, pennies, and tissues found at the crime scenes.

ACTIVITY SEVEN

Learn what really happened to John's bicycle.

Materials

> Student Handout D

Procedure

1. Read the newspaper story provided on page 74 (Student Handout D) to the class. If you wish, you may have students take turns reading the story to the class.
2. Discuss the story. Compare what really happened with the class hypothesis.
3. Explain that comparing and contrasting your hypothesis with what you know to be true is an important part of being a scientist.
4. Did your class identify the cycle snatcher? Why or why not? Discuss why students were correct (or incorrect) in their guess.

Goals for This Activity

> Students will strengthen their comprehension and reading skills as they pay close attention to what happened on the day that John's bicycle was stolen.
> Students will increase their appreciation for the scientific process.
> Students will reflect on their learning before moving on to a new activity.

THE BEDFORD BULLETIN
The Community Newspaper of Bedford Heights

Solved! Students at _____ _____ Use Scientific Inquiry to Solve the Case of the Missing Bicycle

By Samson Case

Student sleuths at _____ School surprised investigators on _____ when they presented clear and convincing evidence that 11-year-old Bedford Heights resident Katie Wong was indeed the culprit who stole John Smith's bicycle on Saturday and left it in a ditch alongside Park Road.

Wong pleaded guilty on _____ after being charged with stealing another resident's bicycle and illegally disposing of it on park property. Wong issued a statement shortly after she was charged stating that she was extremely sorry for taking John's bicycle and she hoped that she could make it up to him.

The Bedford Bulletin interviewed Ms. Wong shortly after she pleaded guilty and learned that a combination of boredom and poor impulse control led the 11-year-old Bedford Heights resident to commit the crime.

"I was walking back from my friend Padma's house when I saw John's bicycle sitting by itself on Jason's lawn. I noticed that Mrs. Sampson and Mrs. Borden were both sitting on their porches, but Mrs. Sampson seemed distracted by her kids and Mrs. Borden looked like she was napping. After reading and doing homework all day, I was ready for some excitement and so I decided that it would be fun to take the bicycle away for a few hours and give it to Padma so that we could ride around the neighborhood together. I went up to John's bicycle and impulsively grabbed it without even thinking twice."

According to student investigators, Wong then tried to ride away on the bike, but the contents of her backpack spilled out on to the ground.

"I quickly stuffed as much as I could into the backpack and then rode away without zipping the bag back up," said Wong. "That's how I must have left all those coins on the ground. I was going to ride the bicycle to Padma's house so that she could take it for a spin, but I started to get scared after I realized that I could easily get caught. I just wanted to have fun. I wasn't trying to get into trouble."

Investigators say that Wong then left the bicycle in a ditch on Park Road, along with her backpack. According to the student investigators that solved the crime, they were able to link Katie Wong to the backpack by examining her handwriting and matching it to the sheet of homework left inside the bag. The student investigators also say that they were able to link Wong to the crime by determining that she had a cold on the day that she stole the bicycle and had left tissues, as well as pennies that she had been collecting, at both crime scenes.

"I can't believe that I left my backpack there," lamented Miss Wong. "I left the bicycle in the ditch because I was afraid to ride it back to Jason's house and I knew that someone would see me if I tried to hide it anywhere else. But, even then, I still got caught! I tried to cover the bicycle with debris but you could still see it through the leaves. I knew that the bicycle was still visible and if I had more time, I would have done a better job covering it up. But I saw Jason and John walking my way and so I just fled. I didn't even notice that I left my backpack at the ditch until I reached my house and by then it was too late. It's too bad, too, because if I hadn't left my backpack with the bicycle, then I might not have gotten caught!"

Appendix A: Crime Scene Footprints

Footprint 1

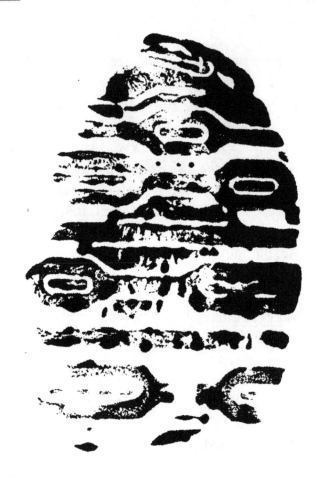

Footprint 2

Footprint 3

© Prufrock Press • *Mystery Science: The Case of the Missing Bicycle*
Permission is granted to photocopy or reproduce this page for single classroom use only.

Footprint 4

Footprint 5

Footprint 6

Footprint 7

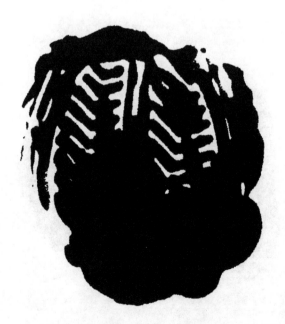

Footprint 8

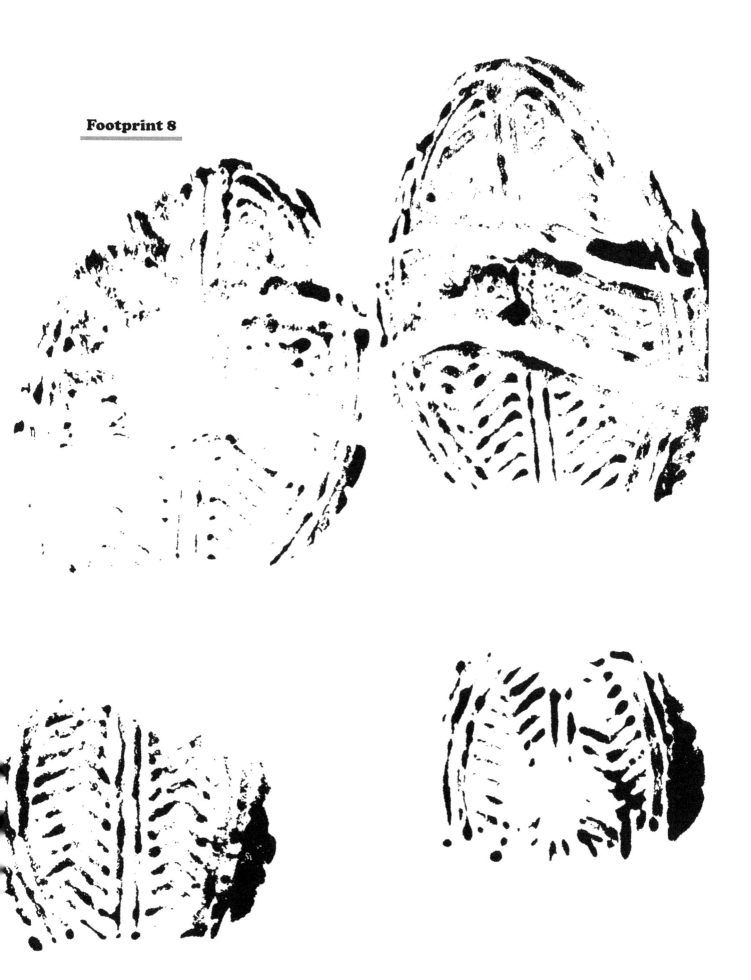

Footprint 9

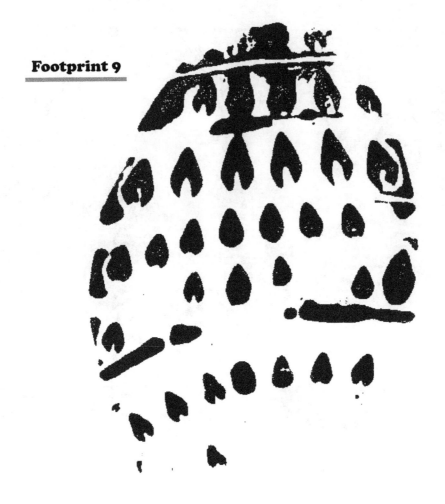

Footprint 10

Name: _____ Date: _____

VOCABULARY

Use your dictionary to look up the following words, and then use each word in a sentence.

Alibi: _____

_____

Artifacts: _____

_____

Assumptions: _____

_____

Clues:_____

_____

Corroborate: _____

_____

Detective: _____

_____

Evidence:_____

_____

Motive: _____

_____

Mystery: _____

_____

Observation: _____

_____

Sequences: _____

_____

Scene: _____

_____

Statement: _____

_____

Suspects: _____

_____

Theory: _____

_____

Appendix C: Rubric

MYSTERY SCIENCE: THE CASE OF THE MISSING BICYCLE

Student Name:	Date:				
ACTIVITY ONE:					
Followed directions by underlining some passages in pencil.	1	2	3	4	5
Followed directions by underlining or circling words that he or she did not know.	1	2	3	4	5
Listened to the story without interrupting.	1	2	3	4	5
Demonstrated recognition and understanding by underlining key pieces of information in the story.	1	2	3	4	5
ACTIVITY TWO:					
Followed directions by quietly observing the crime scenes and recording observations in his or her Mystery Science Detective Notebook.	1	2	3	4	5
Took detailed notes about the crime scenes and used descriptive language that accurately evoked the scenes.	1	2	3	4	5
Accurately recorded multiple details in his or her drawings and neatly labeled each detail.	1	2	3	4	5
Demonstrated superior understanding by circling key pieces of evidence in the drawings.	1	2	3	4	5
ACTIVITY THREE:					
Followed directions by writing measurements in his or her notebook.	1	2	3	4	5
Actively participated in the activity by answering questions, offering ideas, and/or assisting with measurements.	1	2	3	4	5
Showed initiative by volunteering ideas for what you should measure.	1	2	3	4	5
ACTIVITY FOUR:					
Followed directions by offering at least one detail about the crime scenes to the class and by taking notes during the discussion.	1	2	3	4	5
Actively participated in the class discussion by communicating opinions and/or ideas.	1	2	3	4	5
Listened to the class discussion without interrupting peers.	1	2	3	4	5
ACTIVITY FIVE					
Followed directions by successfully completing each task without skipping steps.	1	2	3	4	5
Used station time wisely and answered each question that appeared in his or her notebook.	1	2	3	4	5
Accurately recorded observations and data.	1	2	3	4	5
Demonstrated understanding by making an educated guess about the identity of the culprit.	1	2	3	4	5
ACTIVITY SIX					
Demonstrated mastery by accurately describing the who, what, where, when, and why for his or her guess and by describing how he or she knows this to be true.	1	2	3	4	5
Participated in the class discussion by communicating his or her guesses and/or ideas.	1	2	3	4	5
Total Number of Points (Out of 100)					

Scale: 1: Unsatisfactory   2: Needs Improvement   3: Satisfactory   4: Very Satisfactory   5: Excellent

REFERENCES

National Research Council. (1996). *National science education standards.* Washington, DC: National Academy Press.

COMMON CORE STATE STANDARDS AND NEXT GENERATION SCIENCE STANDARDS ALIGNMENT

Grade Level	Common Core State Standards and Next Generation Science Standards
CCSS Grade 3 ELA-Literacy	RF.3.3 Know and apply grade-level phonics and word analysis skills in decoding words.
	RF.3.4 Read with sufficient accuracy and fluency to support comprehension.
	W.3.8 Recall information from experiences or gather information from print and digital sources; take brief notes on sources and sort evidence into provided categories.
	SL.3.2 Determine the main ideas and supporting details of a text read aloud or information presented in diverse media and formats, including visually, quantitatively, and orally.
CCSS Grade 4 ELA-Literacy	RF.4.3 Know and apply grade-level phonics and word analysis skills in decoding words.
	RF.4.4 Read with sufficient accuracy and fluency to support comprehension.
	W.4.8 Recall relevant information from experiences or gather relevant information from print and digital sources; take notes and categorize information, and provide a list of sources.
	SL.4.2 Paraphrase portions of a text read aloud or information presented in diverse media and formats, including visually, quantitatively, and orally.
CCSS Grade 2 Math	2.MD.A Measure and estimate lengths in standard units.
CCSS Grade 3 Math	3.MD.B Represent and interpret data.
NGSS Grade 2 Matter and Its Interactions	2-PS1-1. Plan and conduct an investigation to describe and classify different kinds of materials by their observable properties.

CPSIA information can be obtained
at www.ICGtesting.com
Printed in the USA
LVHW060523250220
648044LV00019B/927